I0481534

Bitcoin

The Essential Guide to Bitcoin Technology,
Investing, Mining and Security for Beginners

Table of Contents

Chapter 1- What is Bitcoin?

Bitcoin is one of the digital currencies of the world created back in 2009 by an anonymous person who used the alias, Satoshi Nakamoto. In Bitcoin, transactions are carried out without middlemen, meaning that there are no banks. It is known as the first decentralized digital currency since it can be used with no single administrator. The network operates in a peer-to-peer manner where transactions are carried out directly between users, with no intermediary. The nodes in the network take the role of verifying the validity of the transaction by use of cryptography. Note that Bitcoin runs on blockchain technology. This is the public ledger in which all the Bitcoin transactions are recorded.

Physical Bitcoins do not exist, but only in balances kept on the public ledger in the cloud. These, together with all the Bitcoin transactions, are verified using a huge amount of computing power. The popularity of Bitcoin has led to the discovery of various other virtual currencies collectively known as Altcoins.

The Bitcoin balances are kept using private and public keys, which are simply long strings of letters and numbers linked together using a mathematical encryption algorithm used to create them. The public address is available to the world, and people use it when sending Bitcoins, that is, it acts like a bank account number. The private key is the one you must know to be allowed to send Bitcoins, that is, it acts like an ATM pin. It must be kept as a secret because if anyone knows it, they will be able to authorize sending of Bitcoins from your account to another.

How it Works

Bitcoin uses a peer-to-peer network to facilitate instant payments. Bitcoins are created through a process known as *mining*, and the individuals who take part in this process are *miners*. The miners are compensated through rewards and the transaction fees is paid in Bitcoins. The miners are those responsible for verifying the validity of the Bitcoin transactions, hence you can see them as a decentralized authority. Currently, there are only 21 million Bitcoins available. The release of Bitcoins to miners is done in a fixed, periodic and declining rate. The process of mining ensures that Bitcoins are released into circulation. During mining, the miners are expected to solve difficult puzzles after which a new block will be discovered then added to the blockchain and the miner is compensated via payment of Bitcoins. The amount of

Bitcoins paid after the discovery of a new block decreases after every four years. When more miners join the network, and with the discovery of new Bitcoins, the amount of computing needed increases. The mining difficulty also increases.

Initially, during the early days of Bitcoin, a desktop computer was enough for mining Bitcoin. However, after many miners began mining Bitcoin, the difficult increased, making it hard to use an ordinary desktop. To counter this difficult, miners nowadays use faster and more powerful hardware such as ASIC (Application Specific Integrated Circuit) and more powerful processing units such as GPUs (Graphic Processing Units).

Chapter 2- The Origin of Bitcoin

In the early days, food was traded for livestock. Livestock was in turn traded for resources such as maize, wood, etc. After some time, it changed to precious metals such as silver and gold. In this manner, finance evolved.

Bitcoin is a form of money that is evolving constantly. It was developed by an anonymous individual and is under the maintenance of the best technologists in the world. The amazing thing about Bitcoin is that no government owns it or decides its value; it does this on its own.

According to history, the U.S dollar is based on gold. One could go to a bank, give them a dollar and they in turn would give you some gold. When it comes to Bitcoin, it is not based on gold nor silver, but on mathematical proofs.

The generation of Bitcoins is done through a sequence of mathematical formulas running on computers. Bitcoin transactions are added to a public ledger that runs on blockchain technology. Bitcoin is not controlled by a centralized authority such a bank, a country or a government.

Who Created Bitcoin?

The identity of the person who created Bitcoin remains unknown. What we have currently are just speculations. However, the founder of Bitcoin used the pseudonym, *Satoshi Nakamoto*. The accounts under this pseudonym are no longer active and the Bitcoins in them have never been spent.

The domain *Bitcoin.org* was registered on Aug. 18, 2008. However, the identity of the person who registered it is not in public information, so it remains unknown. On Act. 31, 2008, a person going by the name of *Satoshi Nakamoto* made an announcement on The Cryptography Mailing List, in which he/she stated that he/she had been working on an electronic cash system that is fully peer-to-peer and requires no trusted third party to operate. This paper can be found at http://www.Bitcoin.org/Bitcoin.pdf. To date, this paper forms the foundation of knowledge on how Bitcoin operates.

The first Bitcoin block (Block 0) was mined on Jan. 3, 2009, and it was given the name *Genesis Block*. This block has the text "The Times 03/Jan/2009 Chancellor on brink of second bailout for banks," which is a proof that the first Bitcoin was mined on that date.

On Jan. 8, 2009, the first Bitcoin software version was announced on The Cryptography Mailing List. The Bitcoin Block 1 was mined on Jan. 9, 2009, and the Bitcoin mining process began to rise in popularity.

Satoshi Nakamoto is the name linked to the person or group that released a Bitcoin whitepaper in 2008 and worked on releasing the first Bitcoin software in 2009. When signing up for a Bitcoin account, you are only required to enter your birthdate. Satoshi Nakamoto entered his as April 5.

Why did Satoshi Nakamoto choose to Remain Anonymous?

There are a number of reasons why Satoshi Nakamoto chose to remain anonymous. One of them is privacy. The popularity of Bitcoin has increased so much that it has become something of worldwide phenomenon. If Satoshi Nakamoto did not chose to be anonymous, he/she would have attracted so much attention from governments and media.

The second reason why he/she chose to be anonymous is safety. In the year 2009 alone, a total of 32,489 blocks were mined. During that time, the reward rate was 50 BTC per block, which gives 1,624,500 BTC. This is equivalent to over $900 million. One may conclude that only Satoshi and a few other individuals were mining Bitcoin, hence they own the majority of the $900 million. Somebody who owns that much will become a target for criminals, especially considering that Bitcoin is not like regular cash. The private keys needed to authorize Bitcoin payments can be printed, then hidden somewhere. Satoshi chose to remain anonymous in order to limit his/her exposure.

Bitcoin was valued for the first time in 2010. Since Bitcoin was just mined without being traded, it was hard for someone to assign monetary value to units of the cryptocurrency. In 2010, somebody decided to sell their Bitcoins for two pizzas, in which he used 10,000 BTC. If that person only decided to keep those Bitcoins until today, he would be worth over $100 million.

The Rise of Other Cryptocurrencies

With the rise in the popularity of Bitcoin, blockchain technology, decentralized applications and encrypted currencies, and other alternative cryptocurrencies began to emerge. These are mostly known as *Altcoins* developed to help improve on the design of Bitcoin by providing high anonymity, higher speed and other advantages. Examples of such Altcoins include Litecoin and

Namecoin. There are over 1,000 cryptocurrencies in circulation today. New cryptocurrencies are discovered on a frequent basis.

Bitcoin, which was designed with a lack of control and anonymity in mind, has become a target for criminals. This has made many people lose money that they have invested in it. This calls for you to be careful when investing in Bitcoin to avoid scams and theft.

Today, there are numerous platforms where one can spend Bitcoins. This is contributing to its rising popularity. As more uses of Bitcoin have emerged, more money has entered the Bitcoin and cryptocoin ecosystem.

Bitcoin has been described as a promising cryptocurrency, hence a good investment opportunity. There are various ways in which you can invest in Bitcoin. You should identify the best one for you, then venture into it to earn some good money. If you listen to or watch the business news, you will stay updated about Bitcoin prices on a daily basis, which will help you make better decisions about your investment.

Chapter 3- Where can Bitcoin be Used?

For a something to be stable, it must have value. One of the ways by which one can judge the value of a currency is what it can be used for. Most merchants and vendors are now accepting Bitcoins together with or in place of the fiat currency.

One of the first companies to accept Bitcoin was Dell, a computer retailer. After Dell began accepting Bitcoin, it was known as one of the largest company internationally to do so.

In 2015, Dell earned $59 billion. When paying with fiat currency, the fees for a purchase normally ranges between 2 to 3 percent. When using Bitcoin, this fee is lower, and it is almost free. This saves the retailer a lot of money in the future.

The AirBaltic, an airline providing tickets to over 60 destinations in Russia, Europe, Middle East and other chosen destinations, accepts Bitcoin. Other companies such as Cheapair and Expedia are also accepting Bitcoin as a form of payment, not forgetting Microsoft, which is amongst the leading technology companies in the world. You can use Bitcoins to add funds to your Microsoft account and pay for apps, games and other digital content.

These companies have made a very strategic decision to accept Bitcoin as a form of payment in order to incorporate their tech-savvy audiences. Virgin Galactic is another company that accepts payment via Bitcoins. It is a commercial space flight company owned by Richard Branson and includes companies like Virgin Airline and Virgin Mobile. You are allowed to pay for space travel using Bitcoin.

Overstock, a company that sells big-ticket items at a lower price also accepts payment via Bitcoin. It started accepting Bitcoins in January of 2014, making it the first online retailer to accept payment via Bitcoins. It has partnered with Coinbase so that its customers can be allowed to pay for items such as laptops, TV sets and even pillows. For you to be able to pay with Bitcoin on Overstock, you only have to choose the option for "Pay with Bitcoin" and you will be able to complete your purchases.

You can also make payments via Bitcoin on Shopify stores. Shopify is simply an ecommerce website that allows you to create an online shop and sell their products, similarly to eBay and Etsy. Newegg.com, an online electronics retails also accepts payments via Bitcoin. They allow you to purchase electronic items and make payment via Bitcoin. Other companies and retailers accepting payments through Bitcoin include eGifter, Zynga, Subway, etc.

How to Spend Bitcoin

In most cases, making a payment with Bitcoin is similar to sending an email. However, instead of sending a message, you are sending some amount of money to a specific Bitcoin address. The good thing about making a payment with Bitcoin is that no one will require you to provide too much information about yourself. If you are buying physical goods, you give out your name and address. If you are purchasing a digital item, then your email address is enough. If you are making a donation via Bitcoin, you may not be required to provide any kind of information.

Once you have provided the required information, the website will not ask for your credit card information, but it will show Bitcoin payment information made up of the following:

- Link to "Sign in to Coinbase"
- A QR Code

- A Bitcoin address

However, this may differ slightly as determined by the Bitcoin wallet you may be using.

Paying with a Coinbase Wallet

If the merchant you need to pay uses Coinbase when accepting Bitcoin payments and you have funded your Coinbase account, you can complete the checkout by first signing into your Coinbase account then confirming the order.

Once you have confirmed the order, the process will be finished and the merchant will be notified that you have made a payment.

Paying via QR Code

Most processors for Bitcoin payments also provide a QR code at checkout, and this represents a payment amount and a Bitcoin address. QR codes makes it easy for one to make a payment from their Bitcoin wallet app from a smartphone. You only have to scan the QR code and the recipient's Bitcoin address will be pre-filled as well as the requested payment amount. After sending the transaction, the payment will be complete.

This becomes a good choice for those who don't have a Coinbase account or are in need of using a different Bitcoin wallet.

Paying to Bitcoin Address

In case you are unable to scan QR codes or if the merchant only provides a Bitcoin address, then you can manually specify the address as the recipient of the transaction in Bitcoin wallet software. To make a payment to a Bitcoin address, there are two pieces of information you should provide to your Bitcoin wallet software:

- The Bitcoin address of the recipient
- Amount of Bitcoins you need to send

These will then be shown on the payment page during checkout. However, for the case of flexible payments such as donations, the amount will be left up to you. With the amount and address, you just enter them into "send" form of your wallet, then submit the transactions.

In case the merchant uses Coinbase, the checkout page will be updated to indicate that the payment was received a short time after the payment has been sent, and the purchase will be marked as complete. Note: for direct payments and other processors without a processor, the process may differ.

Advantages of Using Bitcoin

When using checks and wire transfers to make and accept payments, several days may be needed for transactions to be cleared. With Bitcoin, this is different as payments can be processed within minutes rather than days. This makes it the best payment option for companies that need to facilitate faster processing of transactions.

When using payment methods such as PayPal and credit cards, a lot of charges are incurred. The transaction fee charged when paying and accepting payment with Bitcoins is low and tends to zero.

Bitcoin is decentralized and no government controls or owns it. This means that no one can take away your Bitcoins. Individuals who have concerns about the mainstream banking system prefer using Bitcoin because of this. After Bitcoin has been sent, it is impossible for one to chargeback. This is not the case when paying via other options like credit card. Criminals have taken advantage of payment methods that allow chargebacks to carry out chargeback crimes. With Bitcoin, this is not possible.

With fiat currency, the government is allowed to print the amount of money it wants. If they print a large amount of a currency, its value will drop, leading to inflation. This is not possible with Bitcoins as there are fixed amounts, that is, 21 million. If all have been mined, then no more Bitcoins will be created. What does it mean? It means that Bitcoin cannot go through inflation like fiat currency. Scarcity is a very important factor as far as currencies are concerned as it helps prevent inflation.

With Bitcoin, one is in possession of his/her currency. When using other forms of digital fiat such as PayPal, your assets are held in an account that may get suspended. If this happens, you will no longer be in control of your fiat currency. With Bitcoin, you are given control of what you have.

Chapter 4- Where can One Buy/Sell Bitcoin?

Buying Bitcoins

The popularity of Bitcoin is increasing every day. At the same, Bitcoin application as well as merchants accepting it as a form of payment is increasing. However, it is good for you to know where to purchase Bitcoins. The following steps will help you buy Bitcoins:

1. Create a Bitcoin Wallet
    For you to be able to purchase Bitcoins, you must have a wallet. This is where you will store your Bitcoins for privacy. You can get one from a site like Blockchain.info or a Mobile App such as Blockchain Bitcoin Wallet for iOS or Bitcoin Wallet for Android. You will be required to fill in some basic details.

2. Choose the Best Trader
    If you don't want to deal with a broker when buying Bitcoins, it is recommended that you find the best exchange. There are several Bitcoin exchanges that you can find online offering a varying performance. Some of these exchanges cannot be trusted, while other are highly limited, meaning that you must be wise when choosing an

exchange. Whenever you are comparing exchanges, compare factors such as the payment methods accepted and the fee charged. Coinbase is said to be the best platform where one can buy Bitcoins, especially when you are buying for the first time. It is easy to use, provides an easy user interface and shows a high consistency whenever it comes to providing customer service; and they don't push their fees too high. Coinbase can be accessed from both mobile and desktop devices. If you are not sure of the best exchange, then it is recommended that you go for Coinbase. Other exchanges where you can buy Bitcoins include CEX, Bitcoin exchange search, LocalBitcoin, etc.

3. Choose your Payment Method

   Most exchanges will accept various modes of payment depending on those they are willing to use. Some payment methods are not highly accepted due to the fact that they are more vulnerable to criminal activity and scammers. Most exchanges accept credit cards and bank account transfers but some limitations are imposed. Wire transfers are accepted in some exchanges, but PayPal transfers are less likely to be accepted. However, Coinbase is different as it allows all of these payment methods, making it the best option, especially for beginners.

4. Buy Bitcoins

   Most exchanges give you information on the number of Bitcoins you can buy for specific sums of money. Note that Bitcoin is volatile in nature, hence its price can vary from exchange to exchange and from time to time.

   It is recommended that you start small then make your trade. After purchasing Bitcoins, they will be stored in an account on the exchange, and this account is generated automatically. After this you should seek a way to transfer the Bitcoins to your Bitcoin wallet address. Note that the exchange may require you to pay some fee for the transfer. Note that Bitcoin transfers may take time. This is because the transaction needs to be added to the blockchain, then confirmed. This may take some time to complete, especially when you are doing it during busy trading hours.

After a successful purchase of Bitcoins, you will be ready to use them. You can choose to sell them, or even use them to purchase something from stores if they are allowed as a form of payment.

Bitcoin ATMs

Bitcoin ATMs allow one to exchange Bitcoins for compatible wallets for cash. While the ATMs are only available in a number of cities, they provide one with an alternative for withdrawing money by use of an exchange. Also, most online wallets and exchanges do not deal with cash directly.

Most Bitcoin ATMs are from companies such as Genesis Coin, BitAccess, Lamassu, CoinOutlet and Robocoin.

Over-the-Counter/Face-to-Face Trades

You can find a local seller and buy Bitcoins from him/her. This is the best option for you if you live in a city and you don't need bank hassles or you prefer anonymity. You only have to visit a website such as LocalBitcoins and find a seller. You will then strike a deal on the site and make all the necessary arrangements. The good thing with the site is that it provides both parties with escrow protection. However, you must be careful when meeting a local Bitcoin seller. Avoid meeting in private places as this is not good for your security. You can also visit a website such as Meetup.com and check whether there Bitcoin meetings held in your area. You can learn a lot about Bitcoin from such a group.

Investment Trust

You may not have interest in buying and keeping huge amounts of Bitcoins. In such a case, you can choose to use an investment trust. A good example of an investment trust is Winklevoss ETF and Bitcoin Investment Trust (BIT). The trust invests solely in Bitcoins and uses modern protocol to keep the Bitcoins safely on behalf of shareholders.

Selling Bitcoins

Buying Bitcoins is a straightforward process, but selling Bitcoins may not be so straightforward. There are various ways you can sell your Bitcoins. However, you have to evaluate and compare them in order to decide on the best method to use. You can sell Bitcoins in person or online.

Selling Bitcoins Online

This is the most popular way one can trade Bitcoin. There are three ways by which you can sell Bitcoins online:

1. A direct trade with some other person, an intermediary who facilitates the connection.
2. Via an online exchange in which the trade will be done with an exchange rather than an individual.
3. On peer-to-peer trading marketplaces where Bitcoin owners are allowed to get discounted

goods using their Bitcoins via other individuals who need to obtain the cryptocurrency with their credit and debit cards.

Let's explore these one by one:

1. Direct trades

   Examples of websites that offer customers such a trade include LocalBitcoins and Coinbase in the U.S, Bittylicious and BitBargain UK in the UK. The sites require you to register as a seller, at which time you must verify your identity. You then create an offer that helps you state that you need to sell some Bitcoins. Once a buyer is found, the website will notify you. While you will then be allowed to interact with the buyer, but you are only required to complete the trade via the website.

   However, when selling Bitcoins on BitBargain UK and Bittylicious, a lengthy process might be involved calling for you to remain patient. BitBargain UK has a very good user support base. Bitcoin users who hold bank accounts in the U.S are advised to use Circle and Coinbase, which have become popular due to their simplicity of use.

2. Exchange trades

You can register on an online exchange and begin to sell Bitcoins. You will still be required to prove your identity and organize the sale. Exchanges normally act in the same way as intermediaries, this time holding funds for both parties. You are provided with a platform where you create a sell order, stating the amount and type of currency you need to sell.

After a buyer places a buying order that matches your selling order, the exchange will complete the transaction on your behalf. After, you will get the currency on your account. However, if you sell your Bitcoins for fiat currencies, you will be required to withdraw the funds to your bank. If there is a delay in the exchange, it will take some time for the funds to reflect in your bank account. It is also possible for you to use a pure cryptocurrency exchange to exchange Bitcoins for other cryptocurrencies.

To be allowed to use some exchanges, you are required to pay a fee. On BTC-e, you will be charged a flat of 0.2%. Exchanges also impose a restriction on the amount of money one can store on the exchange. Despite the restriction, it is not good for you to keep all your coins on the exchange. It is recommended that you keep other funds in your offline storage.

3. Peer-to-peer trading marketplaces

   With the rise in the popularity of Bitcoin, websites such as Purse and Brawker have been started that bring together individuals with specific needs that complement each other. The first category of people are those who need to use Bitcoins to buy goods and services from websites that do not accept digital currencies as a form of payment. The second category is up made of individuals who need to buy Bitcoins via debit/credit cards. The purpose of the marketplace is to bring people with complementary needs together. One category will get complementary goods while the other one will get Bitcoins.

   The marketplace can thus be seen as an intermediary that provides a platform, escrow and Bitcoin wallet for transactions.

   It works as follows:

   1. Millie posts the list of goods she wants to purchase from Amazon as well as the discount she wishes to receive. This does not exceed 25%.

   2. Boss has a debit/credit card and needs to buy Bitcoins whose value matches that of Alice's

purchases. He accepts to trade via the marketplaces, buys the goods and has them delivered to Millie's address.

3. After the successful delivery of the goods, Alice will notify the marketplace and the Bitcoins from Boss will be released from escrow and arrive into his wallet. A small fee as well as the discount Alice had requested will be deducted from the Bitcoins.

Although Boss has paid a higher fee for the transaction, the marketplace has provided him with an easy way of getting Bitcoins via his debit/credit card.

Withdrawing Funds

After selling Bitcoins, you will want to transfer or withdraw your funds. The international wire transfer forms the universal way of moving money around the world. The majority of online Bitcoin markets support this method.

You can also use the Single European Payments Area (SEPA) to send your money to the bank after selling Bitcoins. It was first designed to enhance international transfers between member states of the European Union in an efficient manner. Some exchanges such as Kraken and RTC-e support this payment method.

However, these transfers may incur high charges and take a longer period of time, usually around 4 days, making it expensive to use. Some banks will refuse to accept your request if you need to create an account in order to receive payments from selling Bitcoins. Third party processors can also help you withdraw and receive your fiat funds.

Verifying Identity

In most markets, Bitcoin buyers are required to provide very little identity details. However, Bitcoin sellers are required to provide a lot of detail about their identity. These exchanges require users to provide their details only in anticipation of future regulations.

For you to become a seller, you should complete the identity verification process. After completing it, you will have removed any barriers to selling Bitcoins. The markets will also ask you to upload some scans of 2 utility bills showing your name and address, together with a photo ID. Some of the markets will ask you to upload a photo of yourself while holding your ID and a piece of paper with the name of the market written on it.

Selling Bitcoin in Person

This is the easiest way you can sell Bitcoin. You only have to scan a QR code on the phone of the other person and accept cash-in-hand, making it the easiest way to sell Bitcoin. The process even becomes simpler if you have friends or relatives in need of buying Bitcoins. Help them create a Bitcoin wallet, send them the Bitcoins, then collect your cash.

However, you must first negotiate the rate that works for both of you, then stick to it. If you can't agree on a price, it would be good for you to use the current rate at a Bitcoin exchange platform such as Coindesk or any other prominent exchange. However, some sellers will apply some percentage on the top of these rates as an anonymity/convenience premium. There are also mobile apps that can help you calculate Bitcoin prices. Examples include BTCreport and Zeroblock.

It is always good as a seller to stay updated about the latest fluctuations in the price of Bitcoin. The Bitcoin price normally varies from country to country as a result of obtaining the Bitcoin in relation to the local national currency. Also, ensure you stay safe whenever you are carrying a huge amount of money when meeting in a public place.

LocalBitcoins

This site provides you with a website where you can advertise yourself as a Bitcoin seller to a wide audience. It allows its users to rate one another, meaning that you are able to assess the trustworthiness of a trader. Once you get a reliable reputation, you will be in a position to sell with a premium attached to the Bitcoin price. Here, you are not required to verify your identity in the same way as on other websites.

LocalBitcoins also provides escrow protection services, but these are only offered for online transactions, not for in-person transfers. If someone asks for escrow protection for a face-to-face transaction, you don't have to comply.

Chapter 5- How can Bitcoins be Stored?

You must have heard stories of individuals who have bought Bitcoins then lose access to them once they become valuable. If you are a beginner to Bitcoin, you may be looking for a way to store your Bitcoins to ensure they are in safe and secure storage. If you are holding Bitcoins somewhere, you may need to upgrade to a new store which offers more safety and security.

How Bitcoin Wallets Work

Despite anything you do to secure your Bitcoins, know that you will not be storing Bitcoin itself. The reason is that Bitcoin is not an object, but an encrypted address kept on the blockchain. You only own a unique key that unlocks the specific Bitcoin location, so you need to keep this safe by storing it in a wallet.

This means that Bitcoin wallets store the private keys that one should know to be able to access the Bitcoin address. They normally come in various forms so they can run on various devices. You can make use of paper storage to avoid keeping them on your computer. Also, it is good and advisable for you to create a backup of your Bitcoin wallet.

The Importance of Using a Hardware Bitcoin Wallet

An online Bitcoin wallet provides you with an easy way to store your Bitcoins, or on your computer or smartphone. However, when you expose your Bitcoin wallet to public view, you will be more vulnerable to phishing and hacker scams. That is why it is recommended that you use a hardware wallet that stores your Bitcoins offline.

The majority of hardware wallets look like USB drives and they can easily be connected to computer. They rely on a PIN for security and a secondary password known as a *seed*. This can be used in case one forgets the PIN. However, if you lose both, it is be impossible to access your Bitcoins; and this is why you should write your seed somewhere.

A hardware Bitcoin wallet has a disadvantage in that if you lose it, you will not be in a position to recover your Bitcoins. This calls for you to create a backup of the same on some other encrypted device. If you need to keep your Bitcoins offline, but you are not interested in using a hardware wallet, you can choose to use a paper wallet.

Types of Bitcoin Wallets

Other than hardware wallets, there are various other wallet solutions in which one can store Bitcoins. Let's discuss these:

1. Desktop Wallets
   These are the wallets stored on a personal computer, and they can only be accessed with unique security keys kept on the same computer. They offer a number of advantages compared to online wallets in that they are not as exposed to the public and are less vulnerable to hackers and scammers. Due to the fact that your security keys are less exposed, your wallet remains safe. However, desktop wallets can still be hacked into if the computer gets infected with a malware designed to steal Bitcoins and root out keys.
   An example of a desktop wallet is MultiBit which runs on Linux, Windows and Mac OS X. Hive is also a desktop wallet that runs solely on OS X, and it has some additional features including an app store that can connect you to Bitcoin services directly. Armory is another example of a desktop wallet designed with security in mind. DarkWallet was designed to enhance anonymity, and it uses a lightweight browser plugin to offer services such

as coin mixing, whereby the user's coins are exchanged for others so that people are prevented from tracking them.

2. Paper Wallet

Paper wallets provides Bitcoin users with a secure way of storing Bitcoins, but the users are required to possess adequate knowledge of how digital currencies operate. Paper wallets are generated online using a dedicated website, or even offline for a greater security. Paper wallets do not occupy much space, making it easy for one to store them, and they offer a high level of anonymity. Paper wallets are just a Bitcoin seed that has been written on a piece of paper.

There are numerous websites that offer paper Bitcoin wallet services. On the website, you can generate a Bitcoin address and it will create an image with two QR codes, one being the public address through which you are able to receive Bitcoins, and the other a private address that can be used to authorize transfer of Bitcoins.

When using a paper wallet, the private keys are not stored using digital means, meaning that they are not prone to cyber-attacks common when using other types of Bitcoin wallets.

Note that with paper wallets, there is no way for you to know when money has arrived. The users have to rely on third-party blockchain explorers who can lie and even spy on them.

3. Ledger USB Wallet

    This type of USB wallet relies on Smartcard security and is sold at an affordable cost.

4. Online wallets

    In these types of wallets, your private keys are stored online on a computer under the control of someone else. The computer is connected to the Internet. These services are available, and some are linked to desktop and mobile wallets, meaning that the addresses are replicated on several devices that you own.

    The good thing with online wallets is that they can be accessed from anywhere, regardless of the type of device being used. However, if you don't implement them correctly, the organization that runs the website may become under the control of your keys, meaning that you will lose control over your Bitcoins. This can be risky, especially if you accumulate huge amounts of Bitcoins.

    Coinbase is an integrated wallet/Bitcoin exchange with an online wallet operating worldwide. Users from the Europe and the U.S are able to buy Bitcoins via this exchange.

Circle provides users from all over the world with a way to buy, store and send Bitcoins. It only allows its US users to link their bank accounts to deposit funds, but users from the other countries are allowed to use their credit and debit cards as well.

Blockchain has a popular online wallet known as Strongcoin that provides a hybrid wallet that allows you to encrypt the keys for your private address before you can send them to the severs. The encryption process is normally done on the browser.

Anonymity in Bitcoin Wallets

Bitcoin is completely anonymous. It is also transparent band trackable. Due to these characteristics of Bitcoin, it is referred as *pseudonymous*. Some companies came up with the idea of tracking suspect Bitcoin transactions to "police" the blockchain. This led to the discovery of ideas to counter this and take Bitcoin anonymity a step further. These include stealth addresses, merge avoidance and coin mixing.

Chapter 6- Bitcoin Mining

In the case of fiat currency, the government simply prints the currency when it needs more money. This is not the case with Bitcoin. Bitcoin is not printed, but discovered. Computers from all over the world compete to "mine" Bitcoin.

People on the network are sending Bitcoins to each other. If a record of these transactions is not kept, nobody will be able to tell who has sent how many Bitcoins to whom. To deal with this, the Bitcoin network collects all the transactions that have been done over a particular period of time and assembles them into a single list known as a *block*. The miners are responsible for verifying the validity of these transactions and adding them to the general ledger.

The ledger is a record of the list of blocks and is referred to as the *blockchain*. It can be used at any time for the purpose of determining the transactions that have been made between addresses at any particular period of time. After the creation of a new block of transactions, they are added to the blockchain, thus creating a long list of transactions that have happened. Any miner participating in a particular block must get the block any time it is updated so that they can know what is happening on the Bitcoin network.

However, the ledger should be trusted, not forgetting that it is held digitally. We need to ensure that the blockchain is intact and that no one tampers with it. This is where the miners come to help. After the creation of a block of transactions, the miners put it through a process. They must take the information in the block and apply a mathematical formula to it so that the information can be changed into something else. The result of the process is simply a sequence of numbers and letters, referred to as a *hash*. The hash is normally stored together with the block at the end of the blockchain.

The process of generating hash from a sequence of data such as the Bitcoin block is easy, but it is practically impossible to get the data from which the hash originated. Also, although it is easy for you to generate a hash from huge data, each generated hash is unique. This means that no two different sets of data can give the same hash. A small change in the block leads to a huge change in the hash.

Note that the miners do not use only the transactions contained in a block to generate the hash, but they must use other information. One such data is the hash of the block last added to the blockchain.

As stated above, the hash of each block is generated using the hash of the previous block. With this, it becomes easy for the miners to confirm the legitimacy of a block as well as the block before and after it. If you tamper with the block, then everyone in the blockchain will know.

In case you interfere with a block that has been already been added to the blockchain, its corresponding hash will change. In case a miner checks on the authenticity of the block by running the hashing function on the block, they will realize that the hash is different from the one stored alongside the block. The block will be spotted as fake.

Also, since the hash of a block is used to calculate the hash of the next block, and in case you tamper with a particular block, the hashes of the subsequent will also change and become wrong. This will then be propagated down the chain, making it easy for the miners to spot any fake blocks and remove them from the blockchain.

Competition for Coins

Now you know the process that miners go through to "seal off" a block. The miners compete to do this by use of software designed and developed to be used specifically for mining blocks. Once a miner successfully creates a hash, they get a reward of 25 Bitcoins. The blockchain will also be updated and everyone will be notified. That is the incentive offered to the miners to keep them mining and helping to keep the transactions going.

Proof of Work

The computers are good at producing a hash from a set of data, and the process of doing so is very easy. It is the role of the Bitcoin network to make the process of creating hashes difficult. This is to prevent everyone from creating hashes of hundreds of transactions in a second with all the available Bitcoins mined within minutes. The Bitcoin protocol deliberately makes the process difficult by introducing something known as *proof of work*.

Bitcoin protocol does not access a hash that looks just anyhow. It requires for a hash of a block to be accepted, it must look in a particular way. The hash must have a particular number of zeroes at the start. You are unable to tell how a hash will look like before you produce it, and in case you include some new piece of data in the mix, the generated hash will change completely.

The miners are not allowed to meddle with the transaction data contained in a block, but the data they use to create a different hash must be changed. For them to achieve this, they use a random piece of data known as a *nonce*. This is used together with transaction data in order to create the hash. In case the hash does not fit the format required, the miner has to change the nonce, and the entire thing has to be hashed again. For the miner to find a nonce that works correctly, he or she may have to attempt several, and all miners in the Bitcoin network try to do it simultaneously. This is the process that miners have to go through to earn Bitcoins.

Computationally-Difficult Problem

Mining a Bitcoin block is difficult since the SHA-256 hash of the block's header has to be lower than or equal to the target for the network to accept the block. For the miner to get a hash of a block that begins with the required number of zeroes, they have to go through a number of trials while changing the nonce. For a new hash to be generated in each iteration, the value of the nonce must be incremented.

Network Difficulty Problem

This is the measure of how hard or difficult it is for one to discover a new Bitcoin block compared to how easy the process can be. This must be recalculated after each 2016 blocks to some value in such a way that the past 2016 should have been generated in two weeks if everyone was mining at that difficulty. On average, this yields one block per 10 minutes.

As more miners join the network, the difficulty goes up. If the rate at which the blocks are generated increases, the difficulty also increases in order to compensate, and the rate of block generation goes down. Any blocks generated by malicious miners on the network will not meet the required difficulty target and other miners will be able to identify and reject them. This means the blocks will be worthless.

Block Reward

The block reward is the Bitcoins that a miner earns after successfully discovering a new block. As stated earlier, this is normally 25 Bitcoins. However, this value halves after mining of 210,000 blocks.

Also, the miner is also paid from the fees of users who send the transactions. The fee is paid as an incentive for a miner to add a transaction to their block. With time, the percentage of this fee will become significant.

Bitcoin Mining Hardware

During the early days of Bitcoin, mining could be done with very simple hardware running on a personal computer. However, with the increase in the number of people venturing into Bitcoin mining, the difficulty of mining Bitcoin has increased. This has led to the discovery of new and more powerful Bitcoin mining hardware. Today, it is impossible for one to mine Bitcoin on his/her own from a personal computer. You should choose hardware developed solely for use in Bitcoin mining. This will help minimize your expenditure, especially on electricity. If you use low powerful hardware, you may end up spending more on electricity that the rewards you earn. Below are the hardware components used in Bitcoin mining:

1. CPU

   Initially, one could only mine Bitcoins using the CPU, and the original Satoshi client was commonly used. However, the need to earn more Bitcoins and secure the network have made miners discover many new fonts, making CPU mining futile. You can use your laptop for mining and earn no coin in a decade.

2. GPU

   It was later discovered that the use of a graphics card was a much more efficient way of Bitcoin mining. CPU mining was replaced by GPU mining (Graphical Processing Unit). This increased the rate of Bitcoin mining by 50X to 100X, and the power consumption was also reduced. It is true that any modern GPU is suitable for mining, but the AMD line GPU has been found to be the most suitable for Bitcoin mining.

3. FPGA

As with the CPU to GPU transition, the technology for Bitcoin also advanced to the FPGA (Field Programmable Gate Array). This special hardware was developed solely for Bitcoin mining. It did not being about a huge increase in the processing power like the GPU, but it brought a huge benefit to Bitcoin mining by reducing the power consumption in Bitcoin mining 5X.

4. ASIC

ASIC (Application Specific Integrated Circuit) is the current technology for Bitcoin mining. An ASIC is simply a chip designed and developed for doing one task only. Note that the ASIC cannot be used to perform any task other than the one it has been designed to do. If it has been designed to mine Bitcoins, it can only be used to mine Bitcoins. This has made it increase the mining power up to 100X while reducing the power consumption compared to the previous technologies. There are chances that this technology will mark the end of the disruptive mining technology. This is because there is nothing at the moment or in the near future to replace the ASIC. A refinement will be made to the ASIC products to improve efficiency, but there is nothing expected to increase the hashing power by 50X or 100X, or reduce power consumption by 7X. The ability of this product to consume less power makes it popular for use in mining Bitcoins. It is believed that if you purchase an ASIC device for Bitcoin mining today, it will still be used in mining Bitcoins two years in the future, provided the cost of electricity doesn't exceed the output. Exchange rate also determines the amount of profit earned from mining, but mining devices that are efficient in terms of power consumption are the best for more profitability.

Bitcoin Mining Software

You can mine Bitcoins on your own or choose to join a mining pool. A Bitcoin mining pool is a group of Bitcoin miners who come together to combine their computing power to mine Bitcoin. Most Bitcoin miners choose to join a mining pool because it increases their luck of earning profits in the Bitcoin mining process. Before you join a pool, ensure that you have a Bitcoin wallet to store your Bitcoins. When mining in a pool, the profit earned from every block a pool member generates will be divided amongst the available pool members depending upon the amount of hashes that they have contributed.

If you join a mining pool and use a Bitcoin miner, you will be consuming a bandwidth of 10MB per day. This amount of bandwidth is negligible; however, it will be good for you to have exceptional connectivity so that you may get any necessary updates as fast as possible.

The members of the pool will get a steady band frequent payout (known as reducing the variance), but note that your fee may be reduced by the amount the pool charges. With solo mining, you will get large but infrequent payouts; with pool mining, you will get small but frequent payouts. However, these two will lead to a similar amount, especially if you are using some zero fee pool long term.

Mining software will help you use the mining hardware equipment that you have chosen to use. If you are using

FPGAs and CPUs, you should have a host computer installed with the following:

1. Standard Bitcoin Client
    This is the software that will connect your computer to the network and allow it to interact with Bitcoin clients while forwarding transactions and tracking the blockchain. A significant amount of time will be taken in downloading the entire blockchain to get started. The Bitcoin client is responsible for relaying information between the miner and the Bitcoin network.
2. Bitcoin Mining Software
    This software is responsible for instructing the hardware to do the hard work. There are various types Bitcoin mining software, and you only have to choose one based on the operating system you use.

Bitcoin Cloud Mining

After buying Bitcoin cloud mining contracts, investors are able to earn Bitcoins with no need to hassle with the mining hardware, software, bandwidth, electricity and other necessities of Bitcoin mining.

In cloud mining, you will use mining hardware run from a remote data center. You are only required to have a home computer for communications, Bitcoin wallets, etc. However, you must be very careful when venturing into Bitcoin cloud mining because you can easily fall prey to scammers. Also, the cloud operators will want to be paid, meaning that you may end up earning a low amount of profit. You will also lack control and find the process inflexible.

Generally, there are three types of cloud mining that include the following:

1. Hosted mining
    This involves leasing a mining machine hosted by a provider.
2. Virtual hosted mining
    This involves creating a general purpose and virtual private server, then installing your Bitcoin mining software there.
3. Leased hashing power
    This involves leasing some amount of hashing power without the presence of a dedicated virtual or physical computer. This forms the most popular type of Bitcoin cloud mining.

Determining Mining Profitability

Before purchasing the mining equipment, it would be good for you to determine the profitability you expect.

There are various online calculators that will help you calculate profitability. You only have to input parameters like the hash rate, cost of the equipment, current Bitcoin price and power consumption. You will then be able to know the amount of time it will take for you to see the fruits of your investment.

Network difficulty is also a key parameter that determines how hard it is for one to solve a transaction block, and it varies based on the hash rate of the network.

Risk vs. Reward

Whenever you engage in the mining of any type of cryptocurrency, there are associated risks, but you can earn profit if you make the right decision. When doing the test calculations, you will notice that some Bitcoin cloud mining services are only profitable for a few months; but with the increase in Bitcoin difficulty level, you will begin to make a loss after about four to six months.

It is recommended that you reinvest whatever you have made into maintaining a very competitive hashing rate, which is a highly speculative process. In cloud mining, there is a high risk of mismanagement and fraud. It is advisable that you only invest in cloud mining if you are capable of managing these risks. Before venturing into

Bitcoin mining, talk to your friends and other Bitcoin experts so they may gather substantial knowledge about it prior to your investment.

Chapter 7- Bitcoin Investment

Bitcoin as an electronic currency expected to change the world, but it is a very volatile financial asset. In fact, governments do not recognize Bitcoin as a form of currency. A lot of investment activities surrounding Bitcoin come from traders who hope they will make money from the fluctuations in the price.

The fluctuation in the price of Bitcoin can be dramatic. In 2013 for example, the price of Bitcoin jumped from $40 to $140 within a month. By the end of that year, the price of Bitcoin had reached $1000. It then went back to $300 per Bitcoin. If a currency fluctuates like this, there is a lot of money one can make.

With the increase in the number of ways as well as platforms through which you can get Bitcoin, it is easy to venture into a Bitcoin investment. Let's discuss some of the ways you can invest in Bitcoin:

1. Buy and Hold
    You can invest in Bitcoin by buying and holding the cryptocurrency. You rely on the volatility of the Bitcoin cryptocurrency to buy it when the price is low and sell it when its price is high. This way, you will make a profit. This is similar to trading the

fiat currency. To succeed in this type of investment, you must stay updated on the current Bitcoin prices and rely on Bitcoin charts for a prediction of future Bitcoin prices.

2. Long Positions

Some Bitcoin investors are in need of immediate returns. They buy Bitcoins and then sell them at the end of a price rally. You rely on the volatility of the cryptocurrency to get a high rate of return whenever the market moves in your favor. There are also numerous Bitcoin trading sites that provide leveraged trading, in which the trading site will lend you money while increasing your return.

3. Short Selling

Some individuals may want to bet on the value of Bitcoin going down, mostly after Bitcoin bubble. Short selling in assets involves borrowing the asset at a particular price, for example, $1000, then selling it to another individual at a similar price. In case the price of the asset decreases, for example to $500, you buy it back at low price and give it back to the lender. The profit in this case will be the difference between the asset value when you borrowed it and the asset value when you purchase it in order to pay back the lender.

Short selling Bitcoin can be done on platforms such as Bitfinex where you will find sellers willing to give you their Bitcoins for a certain period of time. There are also derivatives trading sites on which you can do this. However, there is a risk that the market may go against you, so you will lose the money you have invested. This calls for you to know the concepts of margin calls and leveraging before venturing into this type of investment.

4. Regular Purchase Scheme
   If you are too serious about investing in Bitcoin, you might consider devoting a portion of every paycheck to buying this virtual currency. With time, you will have gathered a lot of Bitcoins without incurring a one-time huge expense. With most Bitcoin wallet sites like Coinbase, you are provided with the option of creating regular withdrawals in order to buy Bitcoins.

5. Trading Bitcoin Locally
   You may prefer to keep your money in your local community. In such a case, it is recommended that you consider a service that will allow you to sell Bitcoins to people near you. Instead of searching and connecting with overseas Bitcoin traders, there are online platforms on which you

can find Bitcoin sellers within your immediate locality. However, you must take all necessary precautions whenever you go to meet someone you found online. Meet during the daytime and in a public place; and if it is possible, be accompanied by a friend or relative. An example of such a platform is LocalBitcoins.com. On this platform, you will be allowed to search for Bitcoin buyers from over 200 countries and 600 cities, even the United States.

6. Bitcoin Investment Companies

   Instead of buying then selling Bitcoin directly, you can choose to invest in an investment agency. This option is less risky compared to the former. A good example is Bitcoin Investment Trust which allows its users to buy and sell stock in the same way as any regular company. The company in turn uses the money in buying and selling Bitcoins with the aim of making money to repay the investors. Since the company is involved in buying and selling Bitcoins, the share price of the company is directly affected by the price of Bitcoin in the market. This option is highly preferred by Bitcoin investors because of its simplicity. The Trust hires professionals and experts in the Bitcoin investment field, making it easy to earn profits;

hence the investors are assured a profit. Also, the investor is relieved of the burden of finding buyers as well as managing their Bitcoin accounts.

7. Bitcoin Mining

    Bitcoin mining is a good Bitcoin investment opportunity. In this process, you compete with other miners to solve problems. If your computer solves a problem first, then you will be rewarded some Bitcoins. This gives you the chance to earn Bitcoins without investing your real money. However, for you to remain competitive in this investment, you should have powerful hardware. To ensure that you earn rewards in form of Bitcoins, join a mining pool, where you will share your computing power and be sure of earning Bitcoins. However, make sure you choose a pool that has already established itself in Bitcoin mining.

Earning from your Investment

The following tips will help you earn money from your Bitcoin investment:

1. Buy low, sell high

    The process of buying then selling Bitcoins is similar to that of buying and selling stocks. You can make money buying Bitcoin when the dollar exchange rate is low and then selling it when the rate is high. However, due to the volatility of Bitcoin, it may be hard for you to predict when the price will be rise and when it will fall.

2. Stay updated on BTC market trends

   As stated earlier, it is always hard for one to predict with certainty the direction that the Bitcoin price will take. However, the best way for you to be near certainty is by monitoring the Bitcoin trends in the market. Bitcoin price fluctuates so rapidly, such that the opportunities for making money can appear and disappear rapidly. You should keep a very close eye on the exchange rate to increase your chances of success. There are various Bitcoin discussion forums online that you can join to interact with other Bitcoin investors about trends. A good example of such a platform is Bitcointalk.org. It is important to note that there is no investor or expert who can predict the Bitcoin market with certainty.

8. Purchasing Stable Investments

   You can use your Bitcoin wealth to buy investments that are more stable. Examples include stocks and other commodities. There are various sites on which you can do this. A good example is Coinabul.com that allows you to buy gold with your Bitcoins. You can even choose to sell your Bitcoins and use the money to invest in bonds or stocks. A conservative stock portfolio provides stable and moderate growth and even relatively risky stocks provide lower fluctuation compared to the Bitcoin market. This means that it is advisable to use the money you get from a Bitcoin trade to invest in stocks.

9. Be careful with the amount of money you invest
    When investing in Bitcoin, ensure that you only invest money you can afford to lose. This is normally the case with any risky investment you may undertake. If you earn a profit, so much the better. But what if you make a loss? You must consider the amount of money you invest into Bitcoin, otherwise, you may be left in a financially unstable condition. Your Bitcoin investment can vanish within seconds, meaning that you may face dire consequences if you have invested too much. If you think that you will incur a loss in the future, it would be better to pull out your investment and take a small loss instead of waiting for a major one.

Chapter 8- Bitcoin Security

It is good to ensure that your Bitcoins are safe. In some instances, hackers and scammers will gain access to your Bitcoins. A malware virus can also infect your computer and the Bitcoins you have stored will get lost. After Bitcoins are lost, there is no one you can turn to. Also, there is no way to get back all the Bitcoins you have lost.

When dealing with Bitcoins, you are your own bank unlike with the traditional currencies. Traditional currencies are covered by insurance but Bitcoin is not. However, you should not be scared of this if you want join the Bitcoin network. We only need to inform you about the importance of Bitcoin security and safety. Let us discuss the ways to ensure that your Bitcoins are safe and secure.

Bitcoin Wallet Security

You must have heard stories of people who have lost their Bitcoins while in their wallets. There are various ways to secure your Bitcoin wallet.

1. Encrypt your wallet
   You can secure your wallet by encrypting it with a very strong password. After the encryption, it will be difficult for anyone to access your wallet,

although it will still be possible. Your computer might be infected by a malware, and a hacker can log your keystrokes to steal your password. You must look for ways to keep your password secure. Ensure that you don't forget your password; otherwise, your Bitcoins will be lost. When using Bitcoins, remember that the password recovery options are very limited compared to a bank. You should consider writing your password on a piece of paper and keeping it in a safe location. Ensure that you choose a strong password. A password made up of only letters or easily memorable words is considered weak. A strong password is one with numbers, letters and punctuation marks. The password should be long. The best passwords are those generated by systems developed to do so.

2. Keep your software updated
   When you use the latest versions of Bitcoin software, you will enjoy the latest security fixes. With updates, you can prevent problems of various severity, including having useful features and keeping your wallet safe. Other than the Bitcoin software, ensure that all other software running on your mobile or computer is updated so that your wallet environment can stay safe.

3. Create a back up

In case you keep your private keys in a single wallet, then you lose the wallet or it gets corrupted, you will lose access to your Bitcoins. After backing up your wallet, you should create a copy of the private keys, but it is always recommended that you back up the whole wallet. Some of the addresses may be used for the purpose of storing changes from transactions, and they may not be shown to you by default. It is recommended that you backup your wallet in various places to help you protect it from prying eyes.

If you create an online backup of your wallet, ensure that you encrypt it. This is because online backups are more prone to theft. A computer connected to the Internet is highly prone to attack by malware. That is why we recommend that you encrypt any backup exposed to the Internet.

You should have several secure locations. Avoid single points of failure as they are bad for security. If you keep your backup in several secure locations, nothing will prevent you from recovering your wallet at any time you need. Try to use various media such as CDs, papers and USB keys.

Also, ensure that you create backups of your wallet on a regular basis. This will ensure that all the Bitcoin change addresses, as well as all the new Bitcoin addresses you have created, are part of the backup.

4. Be careful with online services

Always be wary when going for any service that will store your money online. Many online wallets and exchanges have suffered from security breaches. These services do not provide a guarantee that your money will be safe like a bank. This calls for you to be watchful when using online service for storage of your Bitcoins. It is also recommended that you use two-factor authentication to secure your online Bitcoin wallets.

5. Be cautious with the amount you store

Your Bitcoin wallet is similar to a regular wallet with cash. If you know you can't keep a thousand dollars in your pocket, then don't keep huge amounts of Bitcoins in your Bitcoin wallet. It is always be good to store only small amounts of Bitcoins in your mobile, computer or server for everyday use. Ensure that you have secured it well wherever you store huge amounts of Bitcoins.

6. Consider using offline wallets

Offline wallets provide Bitcoin users with the highest level of security for their Bitcoins. Offline wallets are stored in a secured place that is not connected to the Internet or any other network. If you do this correctly, your Bitcoins will be well protected against computer vulnerabilities. When using an offline wallet, combine it with encryption and regular protection and you will have the highest level of security for your Bitcoins.

You can also implement *offline transaction signing*. Here, you have two computers sharing a similar wallet. The first computer should be disconnected from any type of network. This computer holds everything and is capable of signing transactions. The second computer is connected to the network and has only a watching wallet capable of creating only unsigned transactions. To create a new transaction, you must follow these steps:

- Create a new transaction on your online computer, then save it on the USB key.
- Use the offline computer to sign the transaction.
- Use the online computer to send the signed transaction.

The computer connected to the Internet is not allowed to sign transactions, hence it cannot be used for the purpose of withdrawing any funds, even after it is compromised. You can use a wallet such as Armory for the offline transaction signature.

7. Use multi-signature

Bitcoin comes with the multi-signature feature that means that a transaction must get multiple independent approvals to be spent. Organizations can take advantage of this when giving its members access to the treasury. The organization can implement this in such a way that the transaction will only be successful after it has been signed by about 3 to 5 members. Multi-signature wallets are provided in some web wallets so that the user can have control over his Bitcoins while at the same time preventing thieves from stealing their money by compromising a single server or device.

8. Limit how you access corporate Bitcoin wallets

Maybe you run a business and you have decided that you will be using Bitcoin as a medium of currency. However, you must be extra careful whenever you are granting any corporation access to your Bitcoin wallets. Bitcoin is anonymous, hence any attempt to steal your Bitcoins may be hard to detect or track. If any person gains access to your Bitcoin wallet, it will be easy for them to transfer your Bitcoins to some other address without your knowledge. You are not provided with any way to tie the destination wallet to any particular employee.

In the case of organizations where there many staff members where some employees must access the Bitcoin wallet to be able to complete particular transactions, it is advisable that you use those that come with various sub wallets. You should be in a position to sign one sub wallet for each employee who will need access to your Bitcoins, then ensure that you have protected every one via encryptions.

9. Separate the Bitcoins into cold and hot wallets

Hot wallets are those running on machines that have been connected to the Internet. They are referred to as *hot* because they are more exposed to web-based attacks. If you run a Bitcoin online business, then use offline wallets as they are a better option. They are a bit safer and not attractive to hackers. If you are using a web-based wallet, it would be good to keep some of your Bitcoins in an offline wallet.

It is advisable that you keep the majority of your Bitcoins in an offline or cold wallet. This can in turn be kept in a deposit box for safety purposes. You can then keep only a small amount in your web-based wallet - what you will be using for your day-to-day transactions. After receiving a huge amount of Bitcoins in your web-based wallet, transfer them immediately to your offline wallet before they can be attacked by hackers.

10. Keep private keys offline

Each Bitcoin user should remember to remove their private keys from online storage and transfer them to offline storage. Bitcoin wallets normally rely on public addresses for sending and receiving Bitcoins. Private keys are used when checking the balance of Bitcoins in your wallet. They are also needed whenever you need to authorize payments from your Bitcoin wallet. This means that in case one gains access to your private keys, they will be able to transfer Bitcoins from your wallet to another wallet.

To ensure that your Bitcoin wallet is safe, remove your private keys from online storages and transfer them to another location, probably a computer not connected to the Internet. When kept there, it will be impossible for hackers and scammers to access your private keys: they will not be able to steal or transfer your Bitcoins without your consent. It is always hard for malware and hackers to compromise a computer not connected to the Internet.

Whenever you are making a payment for a transaction generated online, you can use a USB stick to bring it offline, then enter the private key on your offline computer. You can then take the transaction to your online computer and complete it from there.

The process may be long and inconvenient, but you should do it for the security of your Bitcoins. Doing this will provide your Bitcoins with an extra level of protection. Wallet protection is very important, especially if you are storing a large amount of Bitcoins in your wallet. The only way to compromise a cold wallet is by gaining physical access to it.

In addition, ensure that you have a backup plan for your peers and family. If you are gone and no one knows where your password and wallets are, your Bitcoins will be lost forever. Make sure somebody you trust knows this.

Other Bitcoin Security Practices

Here are other tips to ensure that your Bitcoins are safe and secure:

1. Use Dedicated Hardware
   You should rely on dedicated hardware when making Bitcoin transactions. When moving data from the online to your offline computer, use a dedicated USB key. This way, you will have minimized exposure to viruses. It would also be good if you dedicate your offline computer to your only offline Bitcoin wallet. This way, you will have minimized the exposure of the computer to web hackers and viruses.

2. Use Linux Operating System
   The best way to move data between an online and offline computer is by means of a USB drive. This will help enhance the safety and security of your Bitcoins. Linux is very good when it comes to resisting USB based attacks, hence you should use it as USB drive when transferring Bitcoins between online and offline storage.

3. Maintain a Secure Offsite Backup
   Your computer may be stolen or get lost, or maybe the hard disk fails or gets destroyed. You will no longer be able to access the Bitcoin wallet, hence

the Bitcoins stored there will be lost. You should create a backup of your wallet and store it somewhere else. It is also recommended that you create several backups and store them in various locations.

Note that it is always good to keep an updated backup for your wallet. In fact, you should back it up after every transaction or every 100 transactions. This way, the backup will be updated with the latest private keys generated, hence granting it access to the Bitcoins.

4. Use Type 2 Deterministic Wallet

   Type 2 Deterministic Wallet is a feature found on both Electrum and Armory open source wallets. The feature uses a seed to deterministically generate all private keys of the future for Bitcoins you receive. With this, you will only be required to create a backup server because the backup will have the seed. In case your wallet gets lost, you will be in a position to use the same seed to recreate the wallet. The recreated wallet will be similar to the previous one since it will have all the private keys as well as the Bitcoins contained in the previous wallet.

5. Use Fragmented Backups

You may only have to create a single backup for the seed, but it is recommended that you create several copies and keep them in different places. In case you are worried about the physical security of your backup, make a fragmented backup. This way, the seed will be split into six fragments and four of them will have to recreate the seed. Each fragment can then be kept in its own place. For a person to be able to access your wallet, they will first have to gain access to four fragments. This is almost impossible. Armory wallet is an example of a wallet that provides its users with the option of creating fragmented backups.

At any particular point in time, ensure that you have direct control over your Bitcoins. This calls for you to make sure that you are the one with direct control over the address where you have kept your Bitcoins.

Storing Bitcoins in an online wallet is a good option as it relieves one from the tasks needed to manage one's own wallets. However, the wallet will be under the control of the exchange and not under your own. In case the exchange is hacked, which has happened with some exchanges, your Bitcoins will get lost. Cases of online hacking and people losing their Bitcoins have been reported. Even if you prefer to use an online wallet, ensure that you withdraw your Bitcoins and leave a small amount in the exchange. If the exchange gets hacked, you will lose an insignificant number.

Chapter 9- Why Businesses Should Accept Bitcoin?

Most businesses are now accepting Bitcoin as a form of payment. Your business should not be left behind. It is a fact that Bitcoin can act as a game-changer for a business. There are various reasons why you should consider accepting this decentralized cryptocurrency as a form of payment. Let us discuss these reasons:

1. Lower transaction fees
    The fees charged per Bitcoin transaction are low compared to the one charged for payments made via debit and credit cards. That is the reason why smaller merchants are opting for Bitcoin as a form of payment. They want to avoid the bigger charges they incur when receiving payments via debit and credit cards.
    Research has shown that smaller merchants usually pay about 2 to 4 percent charges per debit or credit card transaction, not forgetting the hidden fees. With Bitcoin, this can be reduced up to 1%. This means that accepting Bitcoin as a form of payment can make a business reduce it's the transaction costs by 3 to 5 percent. Some Bitcoin

payment processors such as BitPay do not charge any transaction fees.

2. Preventing Fraud

When individuals are making payments to businesses via Bitcoin, they are not allowed to disclose much about their personal details, which provides them with some level of fraud prevention that cannot be afforded with credit and debit card payments. With Bitcoin, the value is not attached to any personal information. It is digital cash that one cannot intercept, and the identity of the user cannot be disclosed.

However, Bitcoin exchanges operated in the US normally collect personal identity information from their users, like names, addresses and bank accounts to establish a Bitcoin wallet.

3. No Chargebacks

A Bitcoin purchase is normally final, so there are no returns or chargebacks like those for credit card dealings. This helps merchants save money. For credit cards, chargebacks occur after the card user disputes a purchase made using his or her credit card, usually because goods were not received or the received defective items. The user might also have fallen victim to theft and not have authorized the purchase.

After a chargeback, the credit card company normally refunds the card owner his or her money from the merchant, and the merchant is also charged a fee. The fee normally ranges between $5 and $15. In the case of Bitcoin, a user who has made payment via Bitcoin will have no option of filing a dispute. Transactions made via cryptocurrency are similar to those made with cash. The transactions are final, which means that the merchant is protected from chargebacks and associated fees.

6. You can get Quick Payments

   For small businesses to succeed, it needs to have cash on hand. Accepting Bitcoin payments puts you closer to cash as compared to accepting credit cards. The problem with credit cards is that your funds may be locked up for about a week or even more, or the funds can be held in escrow in case a buyer asks for a chargeback.

   This is not what happens when accepting payments via Bitcoins. A good example is Coinbase, in which the payouts at the bank account of the merchant come within two business days only. In Bitcoin, settlement is done at the moment of the transaction. Once the customer has paid in Bitcoin, the merchant will receive it immediately and sell it on a website like Coinbase to get back US dollars. They have a guarantee of getting their money.

7. Easy to Accept International Payments
   Independent consultants and small-scale retailers do not sell their services and wares to international customers due to the high fees charged for cross-border payments. With Bitcoin, the cost of doing cross-border transactions is reduced. It makes global payments faster, easier and cheaper. It breaks down invisible borders for a smooth flow of payments. If your business accepts Bitcoin payments from customers from all over the world, they will be reflected on your system at the speed of an email. When receiving international payments via Bitcoin, a retailer can save up to 8% of the transaction fee incurred when transacting via credit and debit cards.

8. Transparency
   Your business may be required to produce documents regarding your accounting activity. With Bitcoin this is easy. Bitcoin allows you to provide information to your members that can be used for verification of balances as well as transactions that have happened. If you run a non-

profit organization, you can allow the public see the amount of money you receive from donations.

9. No Requirement for PCI Compliance

When accepting credit cards online, there are extensive security checks so that one complies with the PCI standard. With Bitcoin, you are only required to secure your Bitcoin wallet as well as the payment requests. Also, you will not have to incur costs as well as the responsibilities required to process sensitive customer information like credit card data.

10. Increased Sales

Accepting payments is one of the ways of expanding your business, reaching more customers and making more sales. Doing so will open your business to international buyers who were unable to access your services. If your business is not accepting Bitcoin payments, you are locking out tech-savvy individuals who rely on Bitcoin to make purchases. If you begin to accept Bitcoins for payments, you will have opened your business to such individuals. This will in turn lead to increased sales.

11. Catering to Consumer Preferences

You might have customers who make payments via credit and debit cards, and they may be sticking to it because you have not provided them with another option. Accepting Bitcoin payments will be a good way to provide your customers with an additional mode of payment. This will also provide them with an extra layer of protection, which is good for their security. This is because with Bitcoin payments, they will not be required to provide many personal details compared to using credit and debit cards.

12. Increase Brand Awareness

You may be running a business that does not need the use of advanced technology. However, accept Bitcoin as a form of payment and see the exposure your business will receive. There are various directories in which you can list your business once you begin to accept payments via Bitcoin. Examples include Coinmap.org, SpendBitcoins.com and weusecoins.com. You may also have your business mentioned on the local news channel since Bitcoin is one of the hot topics in business news all over the world.

Risks of Accepting Bitcoin

Businesses are advised to accept Bitcoin as a form of payment. However, despite the many benefits associated with it, there are also various risks. These include:

1. Bitcoin Volatility

   This is the highest risk when accepting Bitcoin payments as it makes the value of the cryptocurrency unpredictable. After receiving payment in the form of Bitcoins, you will have to look for a way to convert it into your currency of record.

   To avoid being affected negatively by the volatility of Bitcoin, you should convert it into fiat currency immediately after receiving the payment. Examples of platforms where you can do this include Coinbase and BitPay, on which you receive cash from your Bitcoins. When using these services, Bitcoin payments will be done in real time for the current value of the currency. A business is only allowed to hold Bitcoins for a long time for cases of speculative investment.

2. Bitcoin Security

   With Bitcoin, a business can avoid credit card fraud, but the cryptocurrency is not 100 percent safe. Most methods for preventing cyber criminals from accessing Bitcoin wallets are not perfect. It is risky due to the fact Bitcoins are not insured compared to other currencies such as the dollar and the euro.

However, this is changing slowly. Cryptocurrency companies are working in a bid to change this. A company such as Coinbase, for example, holds no more than 2 percent of a customer's digital money online, and in case a breach occurs, the company will insure the losses fully. The fiat currency held on Coinbase is also backed up. However, the security measures will not apply your personal wallet is hacked. This calls for you to secure your personal account, but remember that if the company is attacked, you will still get your funds back.

3. Uncertainty of the Regulations
   Bitcoin regulations are expected to change in the future. Lawmakers are still in the process of crafting laws that will govern the use of Bitcoin. It is our hope that these laws will be stable for the sake of Bitcoin investors. Cryptocurrencies are new, hence no one can predict how governments will regulate its. This even involves the payment of taxes. For businesses to accept Bitcoin as a form of payment, they need to know the tax obligations expected from them.

Bitcoin can be risky once you accept it as a form of payment for your business. However, you can avoid this by securing your Bitcoin wallets and keeping your Bitcoins in exchanges that are insured.

Conclusion

This marks the end of this book. Bitcoin is one of the cryptocurrencies of the world. It was the first cryptocurrency developed by an anonymous individual going by the pseudonym, *Satoshi Nakamoto*. The good thing with Bitcoin is that it is anonymous in nature. When using Bitcoin, you are not required to provide details that identify you directly. To create a Bitcoin account, you are only required to provide your date of birth. Bitcoins are in a Bitcoin wallet. The wallet has public and private keys/addresses. The public addresses is what other Bitcoin users will use when sending Bitcoins to you. The private key is used to authorize Bitcoin payments from your wallet. This means that anybody with the private key can send Bitcoins from your account. The private key should hence be kept as a secret.

To ensure your Bitcoins are safe, void using online wallets: consider using offline wallets because offline/cold wallets are less exposed to hackers and scammers compared to hot/online wallets. After receiving Bitcoins in your online wallets, transfer them to an offline wallet and retain with only a small amount in the online wallet. This way your Bitcoins will be safe.

There are several advantages associated with accepting Bitcoin payments in a business. Amongst these are lower transaction fees, fast processing of transactions and a high level of anonymity.

www.ingramcontent.com/pod-product-compliance
Lightning Source LLC
Chambersburg PA
CBHW071224220526
45468CB00002B/719